ABOUT SECOND CITY POETS

In 2018, after winning the national student competition UniSlam, Sean Colletti, Anne Gill, Hannah Ledlie and Hannah Swingler formed the Second City Poets: a collective intent on creating experimental and collaborative work which pushes the form. Together they were commissioned to write a full-length spoken word show for the 2019 Verve Poetry Festival, and so *Playground* was created. The group's performance at Verve won the Second City Poets a Special Mention in the Sabotage Awards 'Best Collaborative Work' category.

Sadly Hannah Swingler was unable to tour the show, so Kieran Hayes joined the collective and the four revised it into its current form. This book has been produced to accompany their six nights performing *Playground* at the Scottish Poetry Library during the Edinburgh Festival Fringe 2019.

The Second City Poets take their name from the fact that each member grew up in a different place around the world, but each found a second home in Birmingham, the UK's second largest city.

THE SECOND CITY POETS ARE

Sean Colletti is a native of Southern California but has lived in the UK since 2009. He graduated from the University of Birmingham (BA) and the University of East Anglia (MA) and is currently living in Birmingham, finishing his PhD and first novel. He has hosted and performed at various poetry and spoken word nights nationally and internationally. His first pamphlet of poetry, *Saeculum* (2018), was published with Bare Fiction.

Anne Gill is a poet based in Newcastle. She is a submissions reader for Bare Fiction and was shortlisted for the 2018 Outspoken Prize for Poetry. Her poetry has appeared in print and online and she has performed at events nationally and internationally. Her pamphlet, *Raft*, was published by Bad Betty Press in 2019.

Originally from Edinburgh, **Hannah Ledlie** is a writer and poet interested in ideas of belonging, sexuality and dystopia. In 2015 she was shortlisted for the BBC Young Writers' Award, and in 2018 and '19 she was a member of the University of Birmingham's winning UniSlam teams. She was also a member of the winning team at the 2019 Hammer and Tongue national final at the Royal Albert Hall. Hannah is currently Midlands Editor for Sabotage Reviews.

Kieran Hayes is a Nottingham-raised writer and performer who specialises in poetry and theatre. They were part of the Roundhouse Poetry Collective and performed at events such as The Last Word Festival and Citadel Festival and currently co-produces the monthly Speakeasy new material nights in London. They represented the University of Birmingham at Unislam and CUPSI poetry slams.

Second City Poets
Playground

VERVE
POETRY PRESS
BIRMINGHAM

PUBLISHED BY VERVE POETRY PRESS
https://vervepoetrypress.com
mail@vervepoetrypress.com

All rights reserved
© 2019 Second City Poets

The right of Second City Poets to be identified as authors of this work has been asserted in accordance with section 77 of the Copyright, Designs and Patents Act 1988.

No part of this work may be reproduced, stored or transmitted in any form or by any means, graphic, electronic, recorded or mechanical, without the prior written permission of the publisher.

FIRST PUBLISHED AUG 2019

Printed and bound in the UK
by Imprint Digital, Exeter

ISBN: 978-1-912565-31-3

*Mrs Baxter.
The dog really did eat my
homework.*

CONTENTS

London Bridge	10
Did You Know?	12
Crushes	14
Brother / Sister	21
Registration	25
Please complete and return to Mrs Stone by sixth period on Friday	28
A-tisket a-tasket	30
Epilogue	33
Uniform (1)	34
Uniform (2)	35
Uniform (3)	36
Uniform (4)	37
Covering up	38
Games	40
London Bridge	44

Additional Group Poems

I'm sorry, the person you have called is
unavailable right now.   48

Thoughts & Prayers   50

The Sadness Factory   53

Playground

London Bridge

> I wish that I could
> get a fish,
> get a dog,
> get a rat.
> I tried to steal the
> neighbors cat,
> but Mum caught me.

> I got kicked out of
> class for shouting out.
> I don't know what
> they're mad about.
> At least I'm
> contributing now.
> But they don't listen.

> The boys play football
> by the fence,
> by the fence,
> by the fence.
> I'm always distant
> from my friends:
> playing defence.

> My GameBoy is
> about to die.
> I think that I
> just might cry.
> Who will catch the
> Pokémon
> if I should fail?

> I skived a school day
> once again.
> I hope my parents
> don't find out.
> I failed another
> spelling test;
> I'm so stupid.

> I got detention
> after school.
> Third time this week,
> it's what I do.
> I get so bored;
> I don't mean to.
> Then I get distracted.

> The girls play
> happy families,
> families,
> families,
> with mums and dads
> and pregnancies.
> Is this my future?

> Does anyone have
> double-A's
> anywhere?
> I need to play.
> I'll call my dad at
> work and ask if I can
> just go back home.

> I wish my parents
> would get divorced,
> would give me up,
> would go away.
> I think that I should
> run away
> and take my sister.

> I'm glad my parents
> are divorced.
> I just wish I
> saw my mum more.
> She works so hard,
> she makes me proud.
> I hope she knows that.

> The girls don't want
> to marry me,
> marry me, marry me.
> I think they sense that
> I might be
> taking this shit
> too seriously.

> I didn't know Dad
> would say yes –
> didn't know
> I was depressed.
> School didn't teach
> me loneliness (at least
> not on purpose).

Did You Know?

ifyouwatchtoomuchTV yougetsquareeyes
youeateightspiders inyourlife
andyoushouldneverstart asentencewithand
thebesteggs canfloat
ifyoukeepmakingthatface itwillgetstucklikethat
allguyschests aresupposedtobeflat
apinchofsalt makeswaterboilfaster
ittakessevenyears todigestgum
mikessleeping withkatiesmum
ifyouhavesexthen youwillgetpregnantanddie
mikesa fuckinglegend
weonlyuseone tenthofourbrains
katieskind ofstrange
theonlywayyoucanget proteinisthroughmeat
didyouknowyouhave fatthighs
youcansee thegreatwallofchinafromspace
chocolategivesyouspots onyourface
thetongueisdividedintofive areasforthedifferenttastes
nogirlisevergonnafancyaguy thatssmallerthanthem
shakespearedidntwrite anyofhisplays
piercingyourrightear makesyougay
makeup isforgirls
boysdont cry
ifyourereallyquietyoucan actuallydisappear
grownupsare alwaysright

```
M O H V O Q X E J J O S Q I C W W E O N L Y U S E O N E D V
M A K E U P N A N A Y Y N T L A S F O H C N I P A R G C G D
H X D Z E F Z E Y M R T O T I I M F V R C T P A C T J S E X
T T S P Y M Y I B V K U G A Q R M I K E S A Q A Y H D J A S
A A J F G G J D T O N V I K G S A C K Y N Q H L Q E Q N C M
E H N L K B S D V C U I R E K B C P B O P Q U L H T Q S T G
M T L N Y J B N B R R F L S T U B F R U Y C G G N O Q U U M
H E W S A I Y A O Y C Y I S X G K D E E D K H U R N F A A R
G K M Q G C Q T A O N O S E R D G I V A T Q T Y E G Q D L N
U I A O U C N N R U A U E V A N O A A T E T H S T U F R L I
O L H I O W E A E G C K V E Z A Y V H E N H W C S E T S Y U
R K Y P Y V H N A E U E E N A H N U U I T E E H A I R H D K
H C Z K S O T G S T O E R Y P T I O O G H G G E F S A G I M
T U J C E V X E F S Y P G E C I J M Y H O R J S L D T I S K
S T A J K T E R O Q T M O A U W F U J T F E C T I I S H A X
I S N X A H S P R U E A N R B E G M H S O A H S O V R T P I
N T Y X M C E T T A I K N S N C J S G P U T O H B I E T P W
I E O H A U V E H R U I A E L N H E N I R W C A R D V A E B
E G F W R M A G E E Q N F G R E F I I D B A O K E E E F A S
T L H Z E O H L D E Y G A N C T G T P E R L L E T D N F R T
O L I R S O U L I Y L T N A E N E A E R A L A S A I D T V H
R I S A U T O I F E L H C R C E V K E S I O T P W N L Z O E
P W P E P H Y W F S A A Y T A S U H L Q N F E E S T U F J O
D T L T P C F U E W E T A S F A D T S Y S C G A E O O D G N
Y I A H O T I O R T R F G F R D E I S T D H I R K F H T Z L
K X Y G S A O Y E B E A U O U N M W E O U I V E A I S H H Y
G X S I E W Q J N J R C Y G O T L A K D N N E D M V U G B W
S L C R D U Y G T A U E U R Y A G G I I Y A S I N E O I K A
L X E R T O W K T T O Y B F N O R O M G O F Y D E T Y R U Y
R E W U O Y D L A W Y L H J O L A Z S E U R O N T U D S N Y
I R Q O B F H S S Z F V L U I F K O I S C O U T L V N Y S O
G A U Y E I H T T N I C I M M N T K H T A M S W M D A A V U
R S Q G F Z J W E X G K C H C A C W G G N S P R Z P S W B C
O P I N L E M N S B I A T J N C Q V H U S P O I S K O L Z A
F U A I A D M Y Q Z P Q F B T J W S E M E A T T M Q L A A N
S N H C T K D N E G E L G N I K C U F C E C S E I C Q I F G
I W F R U Q W S G G E T S E B E H T F J M E T O V O I N P E
E O M E H T N A H T R E L L A M S S T A H T N O D S Y O B T
U R P I X U M B R G V H I Z I E B S V E F I L R U O Y N I H
A G I P D N I K S E I T A K A V P P B V N A T V E T W V Y B
```

Crushes

Thomas had red hair and freckles,
and blushed whenever someone paid him attention.
He helped me with maths questions
and passed to me in football.
In class he'd borrow my pencils
and scrawl doodles in his jotter.
So I liked him.

Cara was funny.
She made me laugh like I was high.
She was my first narcotic,
I couldn't stop it, I was hooked I wanted all of it.
And she knew that, and she liked that.

Simon looked a bit like Troy from *High School Musical*,
so, I mean he was pretty perfect. And he sang
all the time, even when the teachers told him to stop.
He was so rebellious, so I liked him.

I was short, but Alesha was shorter,
so when we played basketball,
I could block her, because I wasn't sure
if you're supposed to let someone you like beat you.
We didn't listen to the same music -
I was rapping Eminem as she was singing
Blink-182, but I still liked her.

He had the worst singing voice I'd ever heard.
Standing next to him in choir was like
standing next to a strangled bird
but Thomas had red hair and freckles
and he helped me with maths questions.

Once, Simon shared his lunch with a squirrel
so he went hungry and fainted in PE.
But the squirrel was happy. So I liked him.

When Cara laughed,
the laugh consumed her face.
Skin tightened, eyes brightened,
it was frightening how she changed.
She was lightning when we played
and no one could make her laugh quite like me.
And I still believe that's true to this day.

More than once, when we were seven,
I called Alesha's house,
because we didn't have cell phones back then,
and her mom picked up, so I asked if Alesha was there,
and her mom said *Yes, do you want to talk to her?*
and I said *No, thank you!* and hung up,
because I liked her.

Simon asked me to look after his cat
when he threw a house party,
and he didn't invite me to the party
but he trusted me with his cat.

Cara wasn't in my classes, so at the end of the day
I'd wait at the school gates, find reasons to stay.
Pretend I didn't notice her at first - *Oh hey!*
Didn't expect to see you coming through this way.
But I knew. And she knew. And we'd stand for too long and talk.
And I'd linger 'til it got awkward, then I'd linger a bit more,
then I'd go home, log straight on MSN,
click on her name and do it all over again.

I was lucky because no one else had claimed Thomas.
Ella fancied Jack
and Maddie fancied James.
It was a shame really,
that he just had me to like him.

Once I met Simon's parents; we were working together
on a school project and I got to see his bedroom
and he had the same Ikea bed as me
and his mum made us keep the door open
which means she thought that he liked me.
And he offered me water and it was filtered
and he ate with his mouth closed
and his room didn't smell like boys.
So yeah, I liked him.

Jose told me Alesha liked me, but Jose was always talking shit,
so I didn't believe him. So, Jose set up a three-way call
so I could listen when he asked her if she liked me,
and after she said *Yes*, I avoided her at school
for two weeks, because I really liked her.

I never really took much notice of him
and I never wrote letters in my notebook to him
and I never spent lessons looking over at him
but he was pretty good at swimming?
So I liked him.

She was my first kiss, I was definitely not hers.
She had a lot more options than me though,
I know how this works.
She'd call me in the morning, ask to skip school with me,
so I'd get snacks on my way to hers and we'd play Nintendo Wii.
Cara was my crash course in car-crash crushes.
Taught me everything I know about the chase,
and to always wear a seatbelt.

Simon had the best hair. Like the best hair.
Like Daniel Radcliffe in Prisoner of Azkaban hair.
I would do anything for that hair.

Alesha had this gorgeous, blonde ponytail, and I had a
rattail, because my parents obviously weren't
looking out for my best interests.

His hair was alright I guess.
It was a bit messy but it was ginger,
which was cool.

Cara showed me a 5 minute clip of The Mighty Boosh once,
and then I spent the next weekend watching every episode.
From then on our interactions were built on the foundations
of quotes from that show.

And in my dream he was so
dreamy. He smiled at me
and winked, and my god he could wink.
And I had a dream where I died,
and he didn't even save me, but whatever.
But then he was crying so much that
I came back to life and my bridesmaids
were all oranges. So yeah,
I liked him.

I liked how Alesha pretended like she didn't care about
getting good grades in school, but she really did.
And then, once, when we were supposed to write
about a current event in science class,
I got an F, because I wrote about Tony Hawk doing a 900
in skateboarding and how that was, like, physically impossible.
But she thought it was cute, because she liked me.

We never peaked, or met our crescendo.
There was no big curtain call or firework show.
We just started to grow. Separately,
felt like different people going very different ways.
Talked less and less until one day
we spoke to each other for the last time ever.
I didn't know. She didn't know.
This would be the last thing we'd ever say.
It could have been something stupid like *can I borrow a pen?*
But it wasn't. It was a Boosh quote. Whispered call
and response style, bashfully as we crossed paths in a corridor.
And as we so often had, we made each other laugh.
And that was that.

I guess Thomas found out somehow
because when we were put together for Ceilidh dancing
he paused before he held my hands
and kept glancing away during the Gay Gordons.
But us being seen together kept other rumours at bay
so I liked him.

And, I ignored him
so that he'd like me but then
he was ignoring me.

He ignored you?
                              Yes.
Did he pull your hair?
                                       Did he pull your pigtails?
                              Yes.
                                       It means that he likes you.
Did he steal your chair
                                       or your answers in class?
                              Yes.
He likes you.

                    He likes you when he trips you up.
        When he pushes me, he likes me?
                    He pulls your pigtails and he likes you.
        When he ignores me,
                    it means that he likes you
            He likes me when he trips me up.
When he steals your lunch
                    When he hides your pencil case,
        pretends to cut you with your scissors.
                    When he pulls your pigtails he likes you.
When he chops them off.
He likes you.   He likes you.
            When he flicks a lighter in your face?
He likes you.   He likes you.
He likes you so much he pulls your pigtails
        and when he hits you, he likes you.
                    When he bruises you,
and hides your keys
                                He likes you.
When he picks your friends
                    and he takes your phone
                    and gets you drunk
he likes you.
He likes you when he doesn't show up
and ignores your phone calls
        and he really likes you when you go down on him
        and he leaves hickeys all over you to prove that you're his.
He likes you.   He likes you.
                    What did you think pigtails were for?
What do you think you're complaining about – you like him.
            You always wanted him.
            This is what love is.
            He likes you.

                                                    When you want to stop.
He likes you.
                                    When he doesn't stop.
He likes you.
                                                              He's a good guy.
He likes you.   He likes you.   He likes you.
                                You are so lucky.
He likes you.   He likes you.   He likes you.
He likes you so much.   This is what you wanted.
                       He's ignoring me, and he likes me.

Brother / Sister
after 'Trouble' by Cat Stevens

        The cashier asked if we were twins.
        You were always stealing my things.

Always hogging the Super Nintendo.
Donkey Kong Country has two players.

        'Let's play dress up.'
        'Okay. Who do you want to be?'
        'I'm going to be you only better.'

'Let's play *GoldenEye*.'
'Okay. You're going to let me win once, right? Because I'm your younger brother and, like, six?'
'Nope!'

        The teachers never called me by my own name.
        After they taught you,
        you were the one they remembered.

Always asked if I was 'Keith's brother' –
Keith, who got straight-A's and student-of-the-month.

        Once, at my parents' evening, the science teacher
        came up to mum and dad
        and kept talking about how great you were.

When our older cousins were around, I made us all
bologna and mayonnaise sandwiches so they would like me more.

        Jane the pain whose pants are in Spain
        Give me my fucking jumper back.

Keith the Beef, let me be brief:
I only did cross country to be faster than you.

        Do you remember how I'd follow you around
        the supermarket because I was terrified
        someone would try and take you?

Do you remember the first time
you came to me for relationship advice?

        Do you remember me being nice to you?
        Do you remember your first word?

Our first words were en espanol.
¿Recuerdas cuando me conociste por primera vez?

        You never gave me my jumper back.

I beat all your race times and your GPAs.

        I liked when you did my maths homework
        or my science homework. How you'd buy
        me chocolate to make sure that I'd eaten.

I liked when you drove me to school
without Mom and Dad asking you to.

        Do you want to go to the shops?
        I'm hungry and I'm craving bourbons.
        I promise I won't make you pay.

Do you want to listen to music on the way back?
I promise I won't pick Cat Stevens again.
I'm older now and know stuff other than
what Mom and Dad always listen to.

        Did you know that I taught you to walk?
        That I was your first word?

Did you know that you taught me
how siblings and best friends

are not mutually exclusive?

        We would steal bourbons together
        and blame it on each other –
        persuade our mum our brother
        was talking in swear words.
        I was your first word.

We would skip school to go to the
arcade and play *Dance Dance Revolution*.
Everyone would watch us.
I heard them say we looked like brothers.
It felt like we were brothers.

        I used to want to run away at night,
        and, although we had so many fights,
        I always packed for you.

If you ever decide you need to run away,
I have a second bed here, waiting for you.

        I used to hate you, because you were so like me.
        I think that I should call you.
        You are always busy.

I used to hate being me,
which is why I wanted to be you.
I think I should tell you:

Brother,
Oh, brother, I've set you free.
As I find a place
Not to be you, but to be me.

        Sister,
        Oh, sister, you've set me free.
        You have found your place
        And don't want to be like me.

Brother,
Oh, brother, please believe
There's nothing that you can say
There's just not enough here for me.

    Sister,
    Oh sister, you moved away
    I can't hear your voice
    I just wanted you to stay.

Brother,
Oh, brother, I've moved away
I can't see your face
And it's too much for me some days.

    Sister,
    Oh sister why d'you go?
    This place is strange
    Without you hanging out your window.

Brother,
Oh, brother, I can't see.
In every place I check
I have misplaced my memories.

    Sister,
    Oh sister come back to me.
    I need you now
    Stop growing apart from me.

Brother,
Oh, brother, please be mine.
I don't want to fight
Holding back these tears all the time.

Registration

Sean
        Here

Anne
        Here

Kieran
        Here

Hannah   I'm home, I'm in bed
                               I've got flu and an ache in my head.
                               My throat's dry and sore
Sean   I'm tired and I'm bored.
        Here   I wish I was at school instead.

Anne   Time seems to slow
        Here   as I lie under the glow
                               of the luminous stars on my wall.
Kieran   I wish Mum would bring me some toast
        Here   but I'm too weak to call.

Hannah   I move to the sofa so I can be closer
                               to TV repeats of Blue Peter.
                               I stare up at the ceiling, fall into the ether
Sean   see shapes in the cornice,
        Here   the plaster is peeling
                               my eyes start to cross
Anne   as the shadows grow monstrous
        Here   I'm sick and the whole world is reeling.

Kieran   I'm missing the big P7 trip
        Here   but it's not all doom and gloom.
                               When I reach morning
Hannah   the birds sing a chorus
                               wishing me get-well-soon.

Sean
          Here

Anne
          Here

Kieran   The house is empty again
                             I woke up 10 past 8.
                             Leaving is pointless, I'm already late.

Hannah   But trust me, I've not spent this morning in bed
          Here   I've been stalling the warnings and boring ahead
                             I am up and I'm dressed,

Sean   I know what comes next,
          Here   so I'll wait for the bus on the wrong side instead.
                             I'd rather not try than try and still fail.

Anne   Can't fail if don't try, I quit this I've bailed.
          Here
                             They told me I'm a bad kid,

Kieran   so I guess that's it.
                             I don't try to mess up,
                             it's just habit.

Hannah   I can't stand it, it's madness,
          Here   I'm trapped in this sand pit,
                             smashing castles, dashing handfuls

Sean   because I don't know how to handle this.
          Here

Anne
          Here

Kieran

Hannah
          Here   Maybe that's just how it is
                             maybe that's just who I am,

Sean   just a bad little boy
            Here   becoming a full-blown bad man.
                        So I do what you expect,
Anne   play the role that I'm given.
            Here   I've tried changing, being good.
                        You guys are way past forgiving,
Kieran   so why the fuck should I be here,
                        you all gave up on me long ago,
                        so I give up too, I'm off today,
Hannah   I got better places to go.
            Here

Sean

Anne

Kieran

Hannah

Sean

Anne

Please complete and return to Mr Stone by sixth period on Friday

Where were you born?

Do you have any pets?

What are your siblings' names?

Who is your best friend?

Which teacher do you have a crush on?

Who is your favourite parent?

Are you your parents' favourite child?

Do you ever get into the shower, then think, *Oh shit, I'm naked!* - then remember that's the point?

Do you prefer parallel or perpendicular lines?

Do you secretly hate your best friend?

Do you have any friends?

Do you prefer mountains or beaches?

Who is your least favourite Second City Poet?

Why is Anne your least favourite Second City Poet?

Have you ever dreamt you're going to the toilet, and then woken up wetting the bed?

What was the last film you saw?

Have you realised that you probably won't achieve what you want to when you grow up?

Do you know how to file taxes?

Are you scared about the extinction of humanity due to climate change?

If you hate this book will you burn it or recycle it?

What should you be doing right now instead of answering these questions?

A-tisket a-tasket

A green and yellow basket.
She wrote a letter to her love
and on the way she dropped it.

She dropped it, she dropped it
yes on the way she dropped it.
Someone must have picked it up
and put it in their pocket.

A-tisket a-tasket
a green and yellow basket.
She wrote a letter to her love
and on the way she dropped it.

She masked it, she masked it
whenever someone asked it:
                    tell me who is your true love

She'd never ever say it

A-tisket a-tasket
she took her yellow basket
and if she doesn't bring it back
she thinks that she shall die -

                    She writes in third person,
                    trying to hide like a child
                    with her hands over her eyes.

Chapter 1

She was the only girl who played football at break times. The other girls played with hair. She didn't have long hair, which was good because it would have got in the way when she played football.

> She labels her non-fiction fantasy like a bad librarian,
> and when the diaries she labels stories
> cut too close to the core of her
> she puts padlocks on them.

Chapter 2

She heard that Mr Stone had to have a meeting with Alice Smith's parents because he found a love letter Alice had written to him. She thought that was very awkward but the girls said who could blame her. Mr Stone wore nice shirts and a crooked smile.

> Secrets teeter on the tip of her tongue like that child again,
> this time hesitating on the edge of a diving board.
> She's never jumped from this high before.

Chapter 3

Miss Lane had nice eyes and was very kind and said her stories were good.

She got nervous
when she talked
to her.

> Online, she writes under pseudonyms.
> She tells tales about girls who like girls.
> In writing class she tells tales about girls who like guys
> and somehow it always feels like

Chapter 4

She met a nice boy who took her to the cinema and it felt like
                                                                                             lying.

She tells herself

                                           that's all writing ever is

while trying to ignore the knot in her stomach that says

                                          I've still got to believe in it.

Chapter 5

She met a nice boy who took her to the cinema
and it felt like prison.

She decided she would never tell anyone how she feels.
She resigned herself to taking her secret to the grave.
She thought maybe she'd become a hermit
in a cave somewhere, maybe in Glasgow.

But eventually she moved away
and things began to change.

The third person started to shrivel
like paper curling up in flames.

                       We speak in first person
                  without even turning to a page.

Epilogue

These days I think,
maybe it would've been easier
to talk in first person present
if my teachers hadn't talked in future tense
about a husband with such certainty.

Maybe it would've been easier
to write honestly
if not every love story on TV
was girl meets boy.

Maybe it would've been easier
to tell my own story
if I hadn't been wrapped
in such a thick skin
made of a thousand romance novels
each one paper thin.

Maybe the third person
wouldn't still creep up in conversations
where queer rights are discussed like spectator sport
and someone says *gay couples are so adorable*

Maybe I wouldn't feel a hand
around my throat
when I want to shout:

> *Then why are we too scared to come out to you right now?*

>> The third person hasn't left us
>> She still follows us about.

Uniform (1)

They were the colour of everyone else's. Navy Blue.
They were Canterbury of New Zealand tracksuits,

and everyone knew this because the logo was printed on the leg,
as large as shop front lettering.

They had zips that went almost to the hip so you could roll them
into shorts on the one sunny day of the year.

They were a bit dear, but for me they were a blessing,
a fashion trend that wasn't too feminine.

Twenty-five pounds was a small price to pay
for the relief of disappearing.

I used to wear my brother's old clothes.
Hand-me-downs and cast offs,

shrunken tees and stripey socks,
hoodies and pyjama tops.

They were treasures made to measure
thanks to a few stitches by my mum.

These days I dress plain
because grey makes me think
of clean slates.

Uniform (2)

They were baby blue and two sizes too small,
but I still wore them everyday
because I didn't want to admit my mistake,
and I couldn't afford any more.

I've never known what size I actually am, never needed to.
Too baggy or too tight, never wanted it just right.

Bought my first pair of skinny jeans aged 13,
wore them to my first gig later that week.
I've never needed a belt less, but I wore one anyway.

Brand new. Metal studs.
Popped a few off though, so you couldn't tell.

The t-shirt had a logo on, if you can't tell what it is, even better.
I backcombed my hair to make it bigger, it was all that mattered.

Two months later I'm crying as I leave the hairdressers
because it's been cut too short.
My mum asks why it bothers me so much?
I reply *my hair is all I have!*
    ... oh, you sweet summer child.

Uniform (3)

They were the absence of color, because nothing
is more heavy metal than absorbing all visible light.

A collection of T-shirts with
tour dates, graphic album art and nearly-illegible logos
for names like Dissection, Carcass and Rotting Christ.

I wish I could have told people that it was a statement -
that I was living my best, rebellious teenage years -
but I just liked the music

and I learned, early on, that wasn't always the case
from trying to engage with someone wearing a Maiden
or Megadeth shirt who hadn't even listened to them.

And when my heavy metal friends got suspended at lunch
for going into the quad and literally burning bibles, it felt like
Rosencrantz and Guildenstern had turned on me. The corpse paint
washed off when I got home and the trench coat was semi-retired,
only brought out for appropriate fancy dress parties. But the T-shirts
still hung in rotation for years while the music played in the background.

My wardrobe in that house is empty - half in England,
half in boxes - and the rotation now features way more color.
But, on December mornings spent away from my family,
I still don the occasional *Master of Puppets* or *Reign in Blood*.

Uniform (4)

They were frayed and faded. Bracelets stretched
up arms to elbows. I'd put this one on
when my bracelet broke, the one mum got me in Corsica.

I just needed a stop gap until I found another,
so I twisted the handle of a Sainsbury's plastic bag
around my wrist.

Miss Hamnet saw the bright orange in maths class
and tried to embarrass me into taking it off
so I didn't, and it stayed on for almost a year.

It wasn't even one of those reusable plastic bags
that I could have swapped out for a new one when it broke.
I still have it, hidden in a shoebox, somewhere in *dad's* house.

The knot in the plastic is still tight. I still twist my bracelets
around my wrist, and count the beads in the same way
my grandmother did with her rosary.

My mother still sleeps like my grandmother taught her
on her back, like she'd learnt at the convent school,
arms crossed against her chest.

Her daughter would lie in the nightie she'd made her,
with beads under her pillow, muscles clenched,
trying to sleep in a godly manner.

Covering up

Playing along is a skill – one you perfected at lunch table conversations, where the only game boys played was one-upping each other at everyone's expense, pretending it was funny to call Aaron fat or Alex gay. And when you got older and started spending time with girls, they introduced questions like 'If you could change one thing about yourself, what would it be?'; and playing along had to reach new levels when someone answered for you with 'Oh, let me guess. I bet it's that mole on your face.' And you were like 'Ha ha...yeah!' but were thinking What the fuck? Is there a mole on my face? Because you don't start noticing things until someone points them out to you. But they don't know that.

Changing your clothes is a skill – one I perfected in PE changing rooms since before I even knew how my body worked. I just knew that it wasn't right and it needed hiding until it became so, even if it never became so. So I'm the first in, bag checked, shorts out, clothes peg. Long socks. No legs. Tie off. What's next? You see the key to efficient execution, is preparation. So I wear sports tops under my shirts for these very occasions. Because my buttons are undone, my shirt crammed away, laces tied and I am done before anybody can say 'Hey why have you got so much hair around your nipples, what's wrong with you?'

Compensating is a skill – one that requires more work than you bargained for. You're conventionally unattractive. That's fine. You can live with that. It's actually annoying when people try to convince you otherwise, even though you know it comes from a good place. So, you have to try out different things to come off interesting. You're not very funny, so that won't work. You're... smart? You guess? Reading is so much effort, though. Why would anyone read a book? But you do. And then you realize being smart isn't enough. You have to be smart in a way that makes it look like you're not aware you're smart. You have to make it look natural. And you can, because you're used to playing along.

Looking bigger is a skill – one I have perfected in school discos since before I learnt to dance. You gotta play the long game with this one, perfect that upright stance. Shoulders back, hold yourself well. Wear good shoes, nice thick sole, but not enough so people can tell. Identify uneven floors early, position yourself on the correct side. And stop standing next to that Ryan guy so much. He's too tall. Get smaller friends. Spend all your time in public looking at other people and comparing yourself to them. Let it dictate your behaviour, your mood, your life. Let it consume you, because apparently it is that important.

Getting older is a skill – and it's like a matter of becoming someone other than yourself, because you can't get away with doing things how you used to. Can't eat that. Can't drink that. Need to exercise but can't find the time to exercise (but can actually find the time to exercise – just agree to do too many things so that you have a lot of excuses not to exercise). Wake up with new pain in a part of your body that you didn't even know existed until today. Black shirts. Loose jeans. Suck in. Lean forward. Cross arms – maybe it will look like muscle. Wear glasses – maybe it will look distinguished. Dim lights, look in mirror – maybe it will look like you.

Appearing confident is a skill – one I have been working on at parties, in bars and on stages since before I even knew that I hated myself. Be the first in the room to make a joke about yourself, laugh the loudest, be so self-aware that maybe nobody will mention you again for the rest of the night. Wear lots of different hats. But make up reasons for why you're wearing hats. Never tell the truth. Never let your guard down. Never do anything risky. Never put yourself out there. Never believe in anything. Never fall in love. Never tell anyone how you feel. Never feel. Just be someone else. Always be in character as somebody who is comfortable in their own skin, and doesn't care about all this petty superficial bullshit. Do most things purely because you believe the only way anybody could ever actually find you attractive is if you are the most interesting, charismatic and successful person in the world. Beat yourself up constantly for not being that person. But, and I cannot emphasise this enough, never ever show any of this to anyone.

Games

This is a game of Manhunt. You cannot begin until after sundown. The boundaries are the entirety of Navy Housing, which covers the equivalent of three or four neighborhoods with multiple playgrounds. You split into two teams: the hunters and the hunted. It is hide-and-seek-meets-tag on steroids. If you are the hunters and can't climb trees, you're going to lose. If you are the hunted and are better at sprints than long distance, you're going to lose. If it is past midnight and no one has found you, it doesn't mean you've won yet. This is a game of waiting.

In this game players must make their mother proud of them. Not by being the best, but just by trying. Players must show up and be willing to fail, and in doing so accumulate XP in order to grow and unlock new features such as pride and satisfaction. In this game players are not defined by report cards or grades. They are defined by how much they tried. Especially when actually trying seems the scariest thing imaginable. This is a game of failing.

In this game, Player 1 puts on a dressing gown and enters the kitchen. The aim is to stash as many snacks into the pockets of the gown as possible and vacate the room without being caught by another player. Players caught stashing snacks into dressing gown pockets will receive a forfeit, such as being heavily judged or getting told to eat an apple instead. This is a game of greed.

In this game players peel back the outer shell of conkers with chipped nails until they are left with the white flesh. Players must then eat the conkers without getting caught. They must hide them on their tongues. If they are caught they will be taken to the nurse's office and their parents will be called. The players are told this is all for their own good because conkers are poisonous, but it was only Alice who got sick, and she was always sick anyway. This game is called *Sick Days (and How to Get Them!)*

In this game you and Player 2 are in the pool and all the other players are outside of it and throw pennies into the deep end. The player to collect the most from the bottom in one trip wins, but when you emerge with a handful of copper, Player 2 is nowhere to be found. The rest of the players are nowhere to be found, because they've run into the apartment upstairs and you have to play pretend like you found it funny as well.

In this game Player 1 invites Player 2 for a sleepover. Player 1's parents are pleased that Player 1 has a friend, especially one of the same sex. Player 1 is pleased to have got around the no boys in the room rule by not being interested in boys. Player 1 listens for the creak of the stairs. Player 1 doesn't think about what will happen if her parents find out. This is a game of alertness.

In this game, Players 1 and 2 compete against each other to see who can fuck over the other one the most. Player 1 goes first and sabotages Player 2's relationship by inviting her back after the pub, even though she's with someone. Player 2: insert coin. Player 2 sleeps with Player 1's best friend, even though she doesn't like him. High score! Player 1: insert coin. Players 1 and 2 must never be single at the same time, because you can't get to the secret level on Easy Mode. Players 1 and 2 agree to stop playing, but the game never stops, even when the *Continue?* screen reaches zero. The game can always outwait the players.

In this game, Player 1 and Player 2 must attempt to sneak into Player 1's house without waking Player 1's family. Firstly, the players must unlock the huge creaky Victorian door. Secondly, the players must try not to laugh at how ridiculously fucking loud the huge creaky Victorian door is. When inside, Player 1 must pour player two a glass of water without making all the pipes in the house groan and hiss. In bed, Player 1 must kiss the neck of Player 2 while both players try to forget about the rest of the house sleeping in other rooms. Player 1 hopes Player 2 is not just a player. Player 2 is leaving tomorrow, and Player 1 does not want the game to end. This is a game of aching.

In this game, the player to drive the furthest while being drunk gets the most points. Multiply your score by the number of shots you've taken. If you're high, too, double your final score. Bonus points for staying in your lane and not swerving into oncoming traffic. Bonus points for parking in front of your parents' house without hitting the curb. Bonus points for getting the key into the door on the first try. This game is called *Grief (and How to Deal with It)*.

In this game players wear baggy clothes and jumpers. They move their food around their plate, normally clockwise, and talk as they do this. They smile and mix peas with Bolognese sauce. When confronted, players explain that *I actually had a very big lunch*, and that, *no I'm not losing weight, I've actually put on weight*, and that *I have muscles now*, and *I've just come off the pill*, and *I think you're the one with the eating problems*, and *are you okay?* This is a game of diversion.

In this game players must smile at each other. Players must smile and pretend to be happy even though they are not. If they don't do it they will be accused of ruining Christmas, or New Year's, or Tuesdays. This is a game of illusion.

In this game players do not win, they just do. There are no losers. There are no stakes and no high scores, you either play or you do not play. And if you do not play then it does not matter because you are not playing but if you do play then the only thing that matters is that you chose to play, and therefore you are automatically, by default, playing. The intricacies and details do not matter, it is merely about whether you are having fun. Are you having fun? This is a game of perspective.

In this game, Player 1 must try to avoid responding to e-mails from his best friend - because he's 'too busy' - for as long as he can, forgetting Christmas and New Year's and birthdays.

In this game you can customise your character, build them from scratch. They can be as big as you like, you can be 7 foot 2, with swords for arms and three giant horns on your head and wings. And you can travel around the world reaping destruction and gaining attention. And it's fun for a couple hours until you realise that to actually make progress in this game, you need more than that. So you replace swords with skilful hands, and choose a size more suitable to stealth (keep the horns though, because fuck it) and realise how much better you can be with a bit of nuance. You start to appreciate the less obvious attributes and how valuable they can be. This is a game of self-love.

In this game, everyone gets together on the Meadows for New Year's, and one player cries. Whether it's from breaking up or throwing up, one player always cries. Some players try to comfort player one, others pretend to concentrate on the night sky as it explodes above the castle, telling themselves that next year, everyone will be alright. This is a game of hope.

London Bridge

Unpacking boxes
once again –
a new house, but the
same friends.
I used to let them drift
away, but old me,
meet the new me.

I play happy families
with friends I've found
in this city
and Mum and Dad
and Max and me.
Sorry that's really
cheesy.

I met someone who
looked at me
like I'm sound,
the way I am.
It was a short-lived
thing, obviously.
But it got me thinking.

Am I not bad
inherently? School's
just not designed for
me. I'm good at
things, I'm sure I am.
Just need to find
them.

Girls still don't want
to marry me.
But that's alright, I'm
only twenty.
Maybe sometime
down the road? I'll
have to wait and see.

I think that I might
need some help,
think that I'm not
quite well.
I like to spend the day
in bed and ignore my
problems.

> I skived off uni once again.
> No one cares, they won't find out.
> I'm struggling adulting.
> Life's not so easy.

> I wish my problems would go away,
> would not exist,
> would cease to be.
> I think it should be easier
> to be me.

> I wasn't sure that I'd survive,
> surrounded by suicide.
> Surprised to find –
> without trying –
> each year's been an adventure.

> It's okay to be like this.
> It's not my fault,
> I try my best.
> Even though my head's a mess,
> I'm still grafting.

> My final year is knackering;
> I haven't slept since last spring.
> I'm sad and stressed and struggling
> but I'm still singing.

> I'm taking it all day-by-day – an old dog, still wants to play.
> School might have taught me loneliness,
> but I can still learn new tricks.

Additional Group Poems

I'm sorry, the person you have called is unavailable right now.

the person	I am lying on the sofa,	person wrapped
	Wrapped in three blankets.	
is lying	The lights are off.	shut off
	The windows are shut.	
you are right	The door is locked.	locked in
leave today	I could write a three-part	do not
	documentary series on	
do not write	why I do not want to leave	leave
	the house today.	
be part body		you
	Part one would highlight	
part red	all the areas of my body	are circled in
	I don't want to be seen.	
don't	My face is circled in red.	want
	My stomach is circled in red.	
be seen	My wrists are circled in red.	you are seen
there is	In part two, the camera	I'm sorry
	would pan to the television	
nothing	in front of me, but	there is
	there is nothing on.	
in front of	There is only	only static
	the sound of static.	
you		right now
	I could write a three-part	
don't have	documentary series,	but you have a
	but I don't have the energy	
energy		a part

you are	part three, the score would change to horror	in my score
a villain	movie violins, screeching, as my phone turns into	injured person
kill the	a gun on the table, and I am the hero lying	I am stretching
conversation	injured in the street, stretching to reach it	to you
silence the	as the villain approaches to kill the conversation	reach the phone
noise	to silence.	change the silence
do not reach	But the noise goes on.	please
the person		it's me
stretching into		it's me
the horror		it's me

Thoughts & Prayers

Thoughts and prayers...
Thoughts and prayers...
Thoughts and prayers...
Thoughts and prayers...
Thoughts and prayers...
for your thoughts?
Or a hundred dollars
you're going to forget about
hey, at least you gave
sleep at night.
next to a phone just
on all these headlines.
Thoughts and prayers...
Thoughts and prayers...
Thoughts and prayers...
Thoughts and prayers...
Thoughts and prayers...
You give them all your –

Thoughts and prayers...
Thoughts and prayers...
Thoughts and prayers...
Thoughts and prayers...
Thoughts and prayers...
Or for your prayers?
donated to some charity
sometime soon, except
something.
I've been lying
waiting to be turned on
It gets off on all your
Thoughts and prayers...
Thoughts and prayers...
Thoughts and prayers...
Las Vegas, 2017:
Thoughts and prayers...
Thoughts and prayers...

Thoughts and prayers...
Thoughts and prayers...
Thoughts and prayers...
Thoughts and prayers...
A penny
Or a dollar?
or the family of some victim
when you can tell someone,
Whatever helps you
awake in bed
because it gets off
Thoughts and prayers..
Thoughts and prayers...
Thoughts and prayers...
Thoughts and prayers...
Thoughts and prayers...
Thoughts and prayers...
Thoughts and prayers...

Thoughts and prayers...
Thoughts and prayers...
Thoughts and prayers...
Thoughts and prayers...
Sand Hook, 2012:
Thoughts and prayers...
Thoughts and prayers...
Thoughts and prayers...
Thoughts and prayers...
You give them all your –
Thoughts and prayers...
Thoughts and prayers...
Thoughts and prayers...
Thoughts and prayers...
San Ysidro, 84:
Thoughts and prayers...
Thoughts and prayers...
Thoughts and prayers...
Thoughts and prayers...
Did they ever have your –

Thoughts and prayers...
Thoughts and prayers...
You give them all your –
Thoughts and prayers...
Thoughts and prayers...
Thoughts and prayers...
Thoughts and prayers...
Virginia Tech, 2007:
Thoughts and prayers...
Thoughts and prayers...
Thoughts and prayers...
Thoughts and prayers...
Do they still have your –
Thoughts and prayers...
Thoughts and prayers...
Thoughts and prayers...
Thoughts and prayers...
Thoughts and prayers...
Texas Tower, 66:
Thoughts and prayers...
Thoughts and prayers...

Orlando, 2016:
Thoughts and prayers...
Thoughts and prayers...
Thoughts and prayers...
You gave them all your –
Thoughts and prayers...
Thoughts and prayers...
Thoughts and prayers...
Thoughts and prayers...
Columbine, 99:
Thoughts and prayers...
Thoughts and prayers...
Thoughts and prayers...
Thoughts and prayers...
Do they still have your –
Thoughts and prayers...
Thoughts and prayers...
Thoughts and prayers...
Thoughts and prayers...

Thoughts and prayers...
Thoughts and prayers...
Thoughts and prayers...
Thoughts and prayers...
Thoughts and prayers...
Thoughts and prayers...
You'd think by now
are business plans.
we're all about
of happiness
Thoughts and prayers...
Thoughts and prayers...
Thoughts and prayers...
Thoughts and prayers...

Thoughts and prayers...
Thoughts and prayers...
Did they ever have your –
Thoughts and prayers...
Thoughts and prayers...
Thoughts and prayers...
there'd be some bans,
And in the place
that business stuff.
was not supposed
Thoughts and prayers...
Thoughts and prayers...
Thoughts and prayers...
Thoughts and prayers...

Camden, New Jersey, 49:
Thoughts and prayers...
Thoughts and prayers...
Thoughts and prayers...
Thoughts and prayers...
Thoughts and prayers...
but life and death
where I grew up,
The pursuit
to look like this:
Thoughts and prayers...
Thoughts and prayers...
Thoughts and prayers...
Thoughts and prayers...

The Sadness Factory

makes pills like M&Ms and tells you
to take them when you wake up.
If you miss one, it tells you to panic,
and then to take more pills to deal with the panic.

The Sadness Factory gives out inspirational postcards *you're nothing!*
why don't you die!
nobody likes you!
even your dog hates you!

The Sadness Factory prides itself on customer service;
gives out springs that dig into back, arm, sagging breasts
and a bed you can't get out of.

The air in your room is stale but
it doesn't make you open the window.
It even makes wedges to keep it shut
so that you can keep on breathing
in memories as smooth as smoke.

The sadness factory hugs you so tight it's hard to breathe.

The sadness factory must love you
because it always wants to fuck you,

and you love the sadness factory,
you get high off it.

The Sadness Factory covers your bed in crumbs
in case you get hungry later;
it even highlights the calorie information for you
on saver biscuit packs so you don't have to
feel bad about feeling bad about yourself.

The Sadness Factory doesn't want you to get hurt

so it cancels plans for you,

feel bad feel bad feel bad feel bad feel
bad feel bad feel bad feel bad feel bad
feel bad feel bad feel bad feel bad feel
bad feel bad feel bad feel bad feel bad
feel bad feel bad feel bad feel bad feel
bad feel bad feel bad feel bad
feel bad feel bad feel bad feel bad feel
bad feel bad feel
bad feel bad feel bad I can't come out
sorry but I can't

and takes your friends from you when you're sleeping   come out I can't come out sorry
                                                            but I can't I can't come
                                                            out I can't come out I can't come out I'm
                                                            sorry but I
they fall to the floor   can't come out I'm sorry but I can't I'm
                                                            sorry I can't
like soft toys not held   come out I can't come out I can't come
                                                            out I can't I I
tightly enough   can't come out I'm sorry but I can't come
                                                            out sorry but
                                                            I can't come out but I can't come out
                                                            sorry I can't come
it takes anything that could possibly hurt you from you   out sorry I'm sorry I'm sorry but I
                                                            can't I can't come out I'm sorry I I I can't
                                                            come out sorry I can't I can't

It says: *why don't you die?*

55

ACKNOWLEDGEMENTS

Thanks must go to Stuart Bartholomew, who first commissioned *Playground* for the 2019 Verve Poetry Festival. He has continually championed our work and has been very patient with us.

A huge thank you to Second City Poet, Hannah Swingler, who collaborated on the original *Playground* and helped lay the foundations of everything to come.

Thank you to Mikey Barnes, Kimberly Knaggs, and Tian Sewell-Morgan, to the UniSlam community, and particularly Toby Campion.

To Hannah Silva who made us rethink what poetry is.

To everyone who has supported us. To the Birmingham, Newcastle, and London poetry communities. To Writers' Bloc. To our families.

Thanks especially to those who were unlucky enough to teach us over the years.

ABOUT VERVE POETRY PRESS

Verve Poetry Press is a new press focussing intently on meeting a local need in Birmingham - a need for the vibrant poetry scene here in Brum to find a way to present itself to the poetry world via publication. Co-founded by Stuart Bartholomew and Amerah Saleh, it is publishing poets from all corners of the city - poets that represent the city's varied and energetic qualities and will communicate its many poetic stories.

Added to this is a colourful pamphlet series featuring poets who have previously performed at our sister festival - and a poetry show series which captures the magic of longer poetry performance pieces by poets such as Polarbear, Matt Abbott and now the incredible Second City Poets.

Like the festival, we will strive to think about poetry in inclusive ways and embrace the multiplicity of approaches towards this glorious art.

www.vervepoetrypress.com
@VervePoetryPres
mail@vervepoetrypress.com

NOTES...